A Guide for Using

Nate the Great

in the Classroom

Based on the novel written by
Marjorie Weinman Sharmat

This guide written by **Mary Bolte**

Teacher Created Resources, Inc.
6421 Industry Way
Westminster, CA 92683
www.teachercreated.com

ISBN: 978-1-57690-346-9

©1998 Teacher Created Resources, Inc.
Reprinted, 2008
Made in U.S.A.

Illustrated by
Ken Tunell

Edited by
Mary Kaye Taggart

Cover Art by
Wendy Chang

Table of Contents

Introduction

Nate the Great is a determined young detective, who, with an ample supply of pancakes for motivation and thinking, can easily solve any case through inference and deductive reasoning. His cases involve many of his friends and their pets, who have confidence in his abilities as a super sleuth to resolve their dilemmas. Included in this easy reading series are 19 books that encourage young readers to apply literary skills that reinforce their comprehension development as they unravel the clues in each unique mystery. This unit is primarily concerned with the original title, *Nate the Great.* However, we hope that you will also share some of the other titles in this series with your class. The "Appendix" suggests activities for each of the other books in the series. The generic activities on pages 39 and 40 can be used with any of the books.

A Sample Lesson Plan

The "Sample Lesson Plan" on page 4 provides you with a specific set of lesson plan suggestions. Each of the lessons can take from one to several days to complete and can include all or some of the suggested activities. Refer to the "Suggestions for Using the Unit Activities" on pages 7–10 for information relating to the unit activities.

A Unit Planner

If you wish to tailor the suggestions on pages 7–10 to a format other than the one prescribed in the "Sample Lesson Plan," a blank "Unit Planner" is provided on page 5. On a specific day you may choose the activities that you wish to include by writing the activity number or a brief notation about the lesson in the "Unit Activities" section. Space has been provided for reminders, comments, and other pertinent information related to each day's activities. Reproduce copies of the Unit Planner as needed.

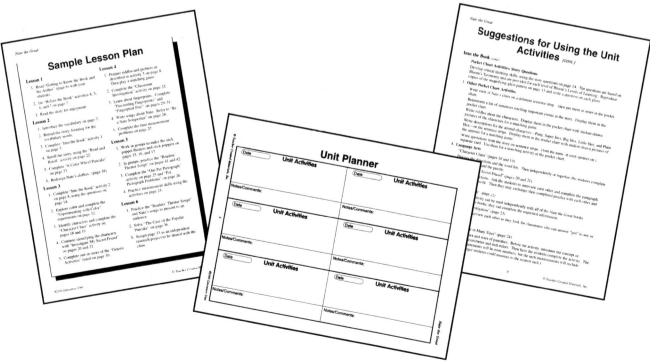

Sample Lesson Plan

Lesson 1

1. Read "Getting to Know the Book and the Author" (page 6) with your students.

2. Do "Before the Book" activities 4, 5, 6, and 7 on page 7.

3. Read the story for enjoyment.

Lesson 2

1. Introduce the vocabulary on page 7.

2. Reread the story, listening for the vocabulary words.

3. Complete "Into the Book" activity 1 on page 7.

4. Retell the story, using the "Read and Retell" activity on page 22.

5. Complete "A Color Wheel Pancake" on page 37.

6. Redesign Nate's clothes. (page 38)

Lesson 3

1. Complete "Into the Book" activity 2 on page 8, using the questions on page 14.

2. Explore color and complete the "Experimenting with Color" experiments on page 32.

3. Identify characters and complete the "Character Clues" activity on pages 18 and 19.

4. Continue identifying the characters with "Investigate My Secret Friend" on pages 20 and 21.

5. Complete one or more of the "Generic Activities" listed on page 10.

Lesson 4

1. Prepare riddles and pictures as described in activity 3 on page 8. Then play a matching game.

2. Complete the "Classroom Investigation" activity on page 23.

3. Learn about fingerprints. Complete "Fascinating Fingerprints" and "Fingerprint Fun!" on pages 29–31.

4. Write songs about Nate. Refer to "Be a Nate Songwriter" on page 28.

5. Complete the time measurement problems on page 27.

Lesson 5

1. Work in groups to make the stick puppet theaters and stick puppets on pages 15, 16, and 17.

2. In groups, practice the "Readers' Theater Script" on pages 41 and 42.

3. Complete the "Our Pet Pictograph" activity on page 25 and "Pet Pictograph Problems" on page 26.

4. Practice measurement skills using the activities on page 24.

Lesson 6

1. Practice the "Readers' Theater Script" and Nate's songs to present to an audience.

2. Solve "The Case of the Popular Pancake" on page 36.

3. Assign page 33 as an independent research project to be shared with the class.

Unit Planner

Unit Activities

Date ⬭

Notes/Comments:

Unit Activities

Date ⬭

Notes/Comments:

Unit Activities

Date ⬭

Notes/Comments:

Unit Activities

Date ⬭

Notes/Comments:

Unit Activities

Date ⬭

Notes/Comments:

Unit Activities

Date ⬭

Notes/Comments:

Getting to Know the Book and the Author

About the Book

(Nate the Great *is published by the Bantam Doubleday Dell Publishing Group in New York and is also available from Doubleday Dell Seal, Canada; Bantam Doubleday Seal, UK; Transworld Publishers, AUS.*)

Have you ever lost something very special and needed a reliable friend to help you find it? Call Nate! That is exactly what Annie did when her special painting of her dog, Fang, disappeared.

Nate's "no nonsense" approach quickly enables him to collect information, question the suspects, and conclude the investigation. His recollection of primary and secondary colors enables him to solve this extraordinary case.

This book strengthens the reader's abilities to understand the strategies of retelling a fiction selection, in that the problem, sequence of events, and solution are evident as the case unfolds.

Nate, in his first case, directs the reader's attention to his role as a private eye who is desirous of happy endings. This story will certainly motivate readers to enjoy the remaining books in the series.

About the Author

Marjorie Weinman Sharmat's family has been a perpetual influence upon her many literary accomplishments during the past thirty years. Numerous characters in her books have been named after members of her family. In the *Nate the Great* series, the readers meet Nate, a youthful detective, named after the author's father Nathan Weinman. Also included are Nate's friends: Annie, named after her mother Anna, Annie's brother Harry, named after her Uncle Harry, and Rosamond, named after her sister Rosalind.

Sharmat collaborated with both her son, Craig, and Rosalind in writing some of the *Nate the Great* books. Her husband, Mitchell Sharmat, is a well-known children's author, and Craig is following in the footsteps of his parents.

Marjorie Weinman Sharmat was born in 1928 in Portland, Maine, and remembers that she was shy, introspective, and enjoyed reading, drawing, and playing the piano. She began writing at the young age of eight when she and a friend wrote a neighborhood newspaper. Her parents inspired her to continue her writing throughout school. Her literary career developed after she graduated from Westbrook Junior College in Portland, Maine. In addition to writing over 100 children's books, she has worked as a circulation staff member in various Yale University libraries, as a greeting card writer, and in advertising.

6

Suggestions for Using the Unit Activities

Use some or all of the following suggestions to introduce your students to *Nate the Great* and to extend their appreciation of the book through activities that cross the curriculum. The suggested activities have been divided into two sections to assist you in planning the literature unit.

The sections are as follows:

- **Before the Book** includes suggestions for preparing the classroom environment and the students for the literature to be read.
- **Into the Book** has activities that focus on the book's content, characters, theme, etc.
- **After the Book** extends the reader's enjoyment of the book.

Before the Book

1. Before you begin the unit, prepare the vocabulary cards, story questions, and sentence strips for the pocket chart activities. See the "Into the Book" section and page 14.

2. Explain to the students that there are 19 *Nate the Great* books. (Display some of the books in the series.) Call attention to the newest book in the series, *Nate the Great Saves the King of Sweden*. The first book you will be reading is *Nate the Great*, published in 1972.

3. Read about the author, Marjorie Weinman Sharmat, on page 6.

4. Set the stage for reading the book by discussing the following questions: What are detectives, and what do they do? Why do people hire them? Where do they usually work? Have you ever acted like a detective?

5. Display the cover of the book. Ask questions about the cover, such as: What do you think Nate is doing? What does it tell you about Nate? What kind of clothing is he wearing? Why does he have a magnifying glass? What do you see in the paintings? Who do you think painted them? What colors did he or she use?

6. Introduce the other characters in the book: Annie, Fang, Harry, Rosamond and her four cats—Super Hex, Big Hex, Little Hex, and Plain Hex.

7. Familiarize the students with the significance of pancakes in the lives of Nate and his friends.

Into the Book

1. **Pocket Chart Activities: Vocabulary Cards**

   After reading the book, discuss the meanings of the following words in context. Make copies of the pancakes on page 13. Write the words on the pancakes. Display the pancakes in a pocket chart. (See page 11.)

Vocabulary Words

detective	pancakes	hex	breakfast	case
picture	solve	monster	paint	bury

Suggestions for Using the Unit
Activities *(cont.)*

Into the Book *(cont.)*

2. **Pocket Chart Activities: Story Questions**

   Develop critical thinking skills, using the story questions on page 14. The questions are based on Bloom's Taxonomy and are provided for each level of Bloom's Levels of Learning. Reproduce copies of the magnifying glass pattern on page 13 and write a question on each glass.

3. **Other Pocket Chart Activities**

   • Write each of Nate's clues on a different sentence strip. Then put them in order in the pocket chart.

   • Brainstorm a list of sentences retelling important events in the story. Display them in the pocket chart.

   • Write riddles about the characters. Display them in the pocket chart with student-drawn pictures of the characters for a matching game.

   • Write descriptions for the animal characters—Fang, Super Hex, Big Hex, Little Hex, and Plain Hex—on the sentence strips. Display them in the pocket chart with student-drawn pictures of the animals for a matching game.

   • Write quotations from the story on sentence strips. Print the name of each speaker on a separate card. Use them for a matching activity in the pocket chart.

4. **Language Arts**

   • "Character Clues" (pages 18 and 19)

   Discuss the directions and the word list. Then, independently or together, the students complete each paragraph and the puzzle.

   • "Investigate My Secret Friend" (pages 20 and 21)

   Discuss the directions. Ask the students to interview each other and complete the paragraph, word list, and puzzle. Then they may exchange their completed puzzles with each other and solve.

   • "Read and Retell" (page 22)

   This retelling activity can be used independently with all of the *Nate the Great* books. As the readers enjoy the books, they can complete the requested information.

   • "Classroom Investigation" (page 23)

   The students interview each other as they look for classmates who can answer "yes" to any of the questions.

5. **Math**

   • "Pancakes Come in Many Sizes" (page 24)

   Discuss the shapes and sizes of pancakes. Before the activity, introduce the concept of diameter, using centimeter and inch rulers. Then have the students complete the activity. The centimeter measurements will be even numbers, but the inch measurements will include fractions. (Younger students could measure to the nearest inch.)

Suggestions for Using the Unit Activities *(cont.)*

Into the Book *(cont.)*

- "Our Pet Pictograph" (page 25)

  Before beginning this activity, survey the students who have pets. Ask about the type and number of pets each student has. Write the survey results on the board. Categorize and list the number of pets for each category. The students will use this information to complete the pictograph on page 25.

- "Pet Pictograph Problems" (page 26)

  Review addition and subtraction word problems. Refer to the Pet Pictograph to solve the problems. When the students are finished, they may write additional word problems, using the pictograph. Have the students exchange their problems and solve.

- "Piano Problems" (page 27)

  Discuss the fact that one hour is equal to 60 minutes. Then have the students decide how many minutes each of the six lessons will last during the hour from 3:00–4:00. The characters may be in any order. Extend the lesson by exploring the class' daily schedule.

6. **Music**

   "Be a Nate Songwriter" (page 28)

   Sing the song, "Frère Jacques." Then sing the song about Nate the Great. Discuss the connections between the problem and solution. The students may complete this activity independently or with each other. Share the completed songs, and put together a "Nate Songbook."

7. **Science**

   - "Fascinating Fingerprints" (page 29) and "Fingerprint Fun!" (pages 30 and 31)

     Together, read and review the fingerprint information while observing your own fingertips. Then complete the activity and help the students match the three patterns, arch, loop, and whorl, to their own fingerprints. Share and discuss the results. Were most prints loops? Did anyone have arches?

   - "Experimenting with Color" (page 32)

     Review primary and secondary colors. Then do both experiments and record the procedure on the experiment form on page 33. The second experiment can be done in connection with "A Color Wheel Pancake" on page 37.

   - "Science Fun with Nate the Great" (page 33)

     Use this form with the experiments in this unit. It can also be used in any future experiments related to the *Nate the Great* books.

8. **Social Studies**

   - "Pancakes Around the World" (page 34) and "Pancakes Around the World—Reference Guide" (page 35)

     Read and discuss the pancake information with the students. Locate the different countries on a map while learning about flat, rolled, and folded pancakes. Refer to the "Related Pancake Books" section on page 44.

Suggestions for Using the Unit
Activities *(cont.)*

Into the Book *(cont.)*

- "The Case of the Popular Pancake" (page 36)

  After discussing "Pancakes Around the World," have the students choose one of the kinds of pancakes to research. This activity may be completed independently or as a group.

9. **Art**

- "A Color Wheel Pancake" (page 37)

  This activity can be done simultaneously with the second experiment on page 32 or separately. Refer to page 44 for books about color.

- "Nate Needs Some New Clothes!" (page 38)

  Examine and discuss Nate's traditional detective clothing and how it could be more attractive. Redesign his suit with new colors, patterns, etc.

10. **Generic Activities**

- "Super, Big, Little, and Plain" (page 39)

  Brainstorm things that are super, big, and little in size and others that are plain in appearance. Then finish the activity by sharing the results.

- "New Character Clues" (page 40)

Use this form for the characters introduced in the other Nate the Great books: Esmeralda, Oliver, Sludge, Claude, Finley, Pip, etc.

After the Book

Culminating Activity

"Readers' Theater Script" (pages 41 and 42)

Provide a copy of the script for each performer. You may wish to highlight the parts and laminate the scripts before distributing them. In groups, students can choose or be assigned parts. Practice reading the script together. When the performers are ready to make a presentation to an audience, have them stand in a line or semicircle to perform.

Variations for Performance

- –There can be two casts. One reads while the other performs the actions of the characters or manipulates stick puppets.

- –All performers can stand with their backs to the audience. When a performer reads his or her lines, he or she turns, faces the audience, and reads the lines. When finished, he or she faces away from the audience again.

- –Make masks for the characters.

- –Make decorative name tags which look like color wheels to identify the readers.

Pocket Chart Activities

Prepare a pocket chart for storing and using the vocabulary cards, the question cards, and the sentence strips.

How to Make a Pocket Chart

If a commercial pocket chart is unavailable, you can make a pocket chart if you have access to a laminator. Begin by laminating a 24" x 36" (60 cm x 90 cm) piece of colored tagboard. Run about 20" (50 cm) of additional plastic. To make nine pockets, cut the clear plastic into nine equal strips. Space the strips equally down the 36" (90 cm) length of the tagboard. Attach each strip with cellophane tape along the sides and bottom. This will hold the sentence strips, word cards, etc., and can be displayed in a learning center or mounted on a chalk tray for use with a group. When your pocket chart is ready, use it to display sentence strips, vocabulary words, and question cards. A sample chart is provided below.

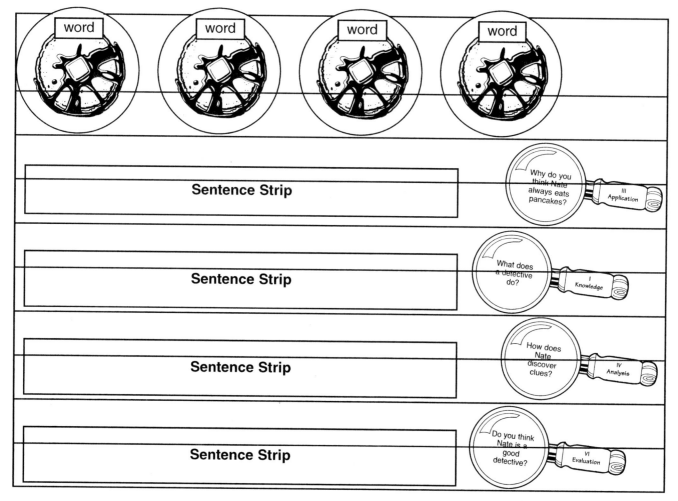

How to Use the Pocket Chart

1. On light brown or tan paper, reproduce the pancake pattern on page 13. Make vocabulary cards as directed on page 7. Print the definitions on sentence strips for a matching activity.

Pocket Chart Activities *(cont.)*

2. Print the names of the characters—Nate, Annie, Harry, Rosamond, Fang, Super Hex, Big Hex, Little Hex, and Plain Hex—on separate sentence strips. Match each vocabulary word to the character or characters with whom the word can be associated.

3. Print the events from the story on sentence strips. Have the students display them in sequential order.

4. Print the clues to the mystery that Nate is trying to solve on sentence strips. Then have the students display them in sequential order.

5. Reproduce the magnifying glass pattern on page 13. Write a Bloom's Level of Learning on each handle and a story question from page 14 on the lens.

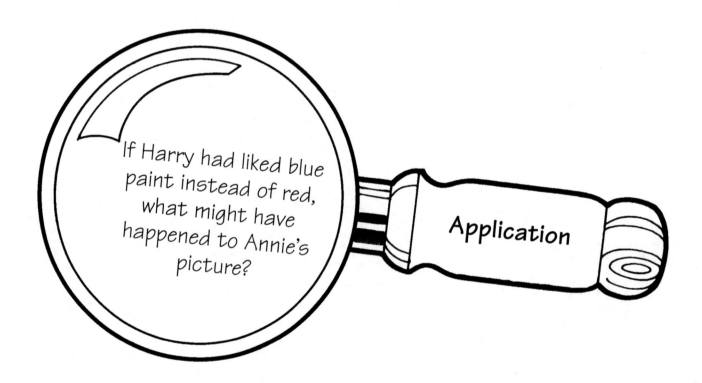

If Harry had liked blue paint instead of red, what might have happened to Annie's picture?

Application

6. Use the magnifying glass cards after reading the story. These will provide opportunities for the students to develop and practice higher-level critical thinking skills.

7. Have a student choose a card and read it aloud or give it to the teacher to read aloud. Have the student answer the question or call on a volunteer to answer it.

8. Arrange the students in pairs. Read the questions and ask the partners to take turns answering them.

9. Play a game. Divide the class into two teams. Ask for a response to a question written on one of the cards. Score a point for each appropriate response. If the question cards have been prepared for several different *Nate the Great* books, mix up the cards and ask the team members to respond by also naming the book that relates to the question. Extra points can be awarded for this.

Pocket Chart Patterns

See page 12 for directions.

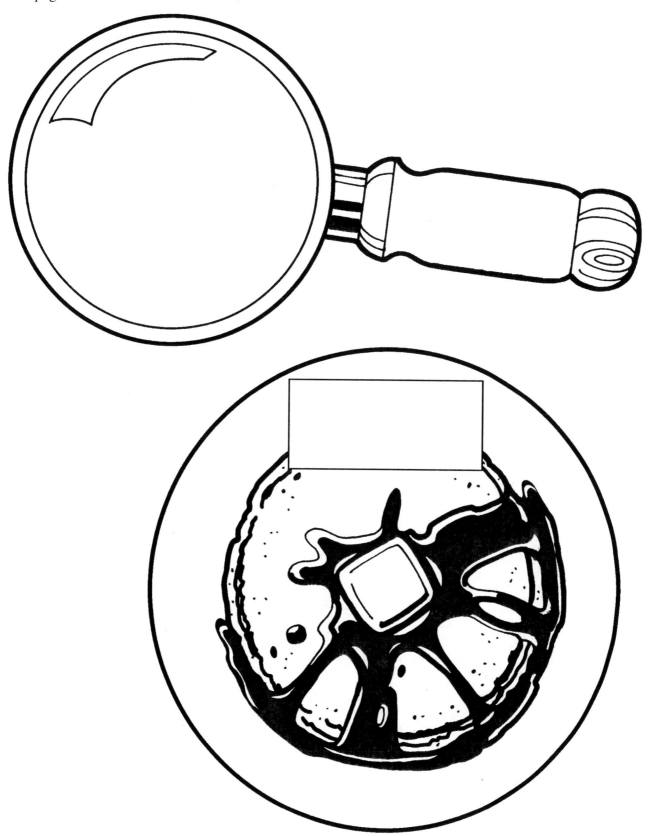

Story Questions

Use the following questions for the suggested activities on page 8. Make copies of the magnifying glass pattern on page 13 and cut them out. Write a question on each of the magnifying glasses.

I. KNOWLEDGE (ability to recall learned information)
- Who was Nate the Great?
- What does a detective do?
- What was the case that Nate had to solve in this book?
- What food did Nate, Annie, Rosamond, and Harry like to eat?

II. COMPREHENSION (ability to master basic understanding of information)
- Why did Nate think that Fang may have taken Annie's picture?
- What convinced Nate that Rosamond had not taken the picture?
- When Nate looked at Harry's paintings, what clues did he have that Harry had painted the picture?

III. APPLICATION (ability to do something new with information)
- If Harry had liked blue paint instead of red, what might have happened to Annie's picture?
- How do you think Nate would have felt if Rosamond had had four dogs instead of four cats?
- Why do you think Nate always eats pancakes?

IV. ANALYSIS (ability to examine the parts of a whole)
- When Annie told Nate that she wanted him to come back and see her new painting of Fang, why did Nate say, "If Harry doesn't see it first"?
- Why do you think Rosamond's cats all have the name Hex?
- How does Nate discover clues?
- Why do you think Harry painted over Annie's picture of Fang?

V. SYNTHESIS (ability to bring together information to make something new)
- What do you think Annie will do with her next painting of Fang?
- Do you think Harry would have ever told Annie and Nate that he had painted over Fang's picture? Why?
- What do you think Nate will write in his note to his mother when he returns to see her next painting of Fang?

VI. EVALUATION (ability to form and defend an opinion)
- Do you think Nate is a good detective? Why or why not?
- Would you call Nate to solve a case for you? Why or why not?
- If Harry had been your little brother, would you have forgiven him? Why or why not?
- Are you ready to read another book about a case that Nate has to solve? Why or why not?

Stick Puppet Theaters

Make a class set of puppet theaters (one for each student) or make one theater for every two to four students. The patterns and directions for making the stick puppets are on pages 16 and 17.

Materials:

- 22" x 28" (56 cm x 71 cm) pieces of colored poster board (enough for each student or group of students)

- markers, crayons, or paints

- scissors or a craft knife

Directions: Fold the poster board 8" (20 cm) in from each of the shorter sides. (See the picture below.) Cut a "window" in the front panel, large enough to accommodate two or three stick puppets. Let the children personalize and decorate their own theaters. Laminate the stick puppet theaters to make them more durable. You may wish to send the theaters home at the end of the year or save them to use year after year.

Consider the following suggestions for using the puppets and the puppet theaters:

- Prepare the stick puppets, using the directions on page 16. Use the puppets and the puppet theaters with the "Readers' Theater Script" on pages 41 and 42. (Let small groups of students take turns reading the parts and using the stick puppets.)

- Let the students experiment with the puppets by telling the story in their own words or reading from the book.

- Read quotations from the book or make statements about the characters and ask the students to hold up the stick puppets represented by the quotes or statements.

Stick Puppet Patterns

Directions: Reproduce the patterns on tagboard or construction paper. Have students color the patterns. Cut them along the dashed lines. To complete the stick puppets, glue each pattern to a tongue depressor or a craft stick. Use the stick puppets with puppet theaters and/or the "Readers' Theater Script."

Stick Puppet Patterns *(cont.)*

See page 16 for directions.

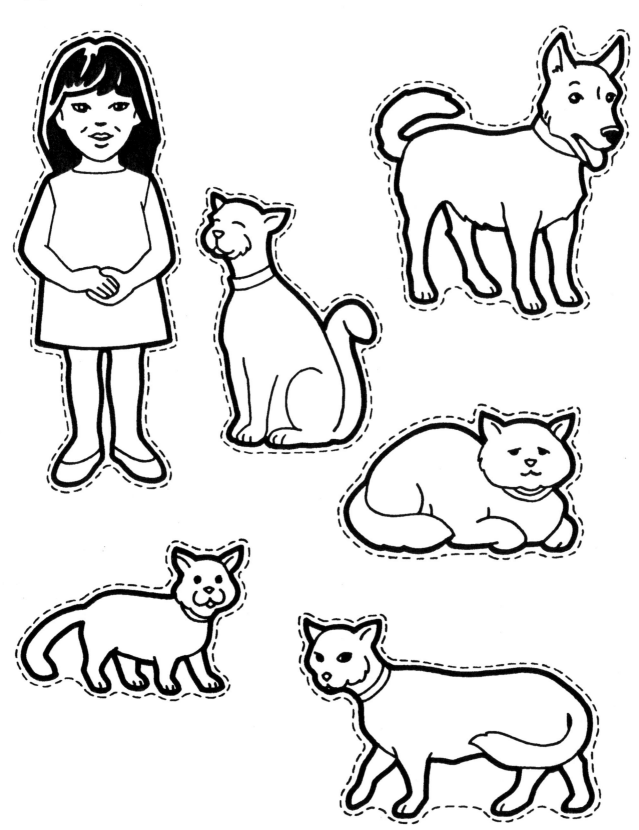

Name _____

Character Clues

Read the paragraphs about Nate, Annie, Harry, and Rosamond. Choose the correct missing words from the list below that describe these characters, and write the words in the blanks. Then find the words in the word search puzzle on the next page. The words may go up, down, across, or diagonally. Circle each word when you find it. (Words may be used more than once.)

Word List

Annie	**eyes**	**Little**	**pancakes**
Big	**Nate**	**monster**	**Plain**
black	**Fang**	**note**	**red**
case	**friend**	**orange**	**Super**
detective	**Harry**	**paint**	**yellow**

1. _____ the Great is a famous_____. He likes to

   eat_____. Whenever he goes out on a_____, he

   writes a_____to his mother so that she knows where he is

   going. His good friend is_____.

2. _____likes to_____pictures. Her favorite color

   is_____. She has a little brother named_____and

   a dog named_____. She likes to eat_____.

3. _____is Annie's little brother. His favorite color

   is_____. He painted a red_____with three heads.

   The monster turned out_____because he painted

   the_____monster over the_____dog. Harry also

   likes to eat_____.

Name _____

Character Clues (cont.)

4. Rosamond is a_____of Annie's. She has

_____hair and green_____. Her four cats are

named_____Hex,_____Hex,_____

Hex, and_____Hex. Rosamond also likes to

eat_____.

Be a super sleuth and find the words!

```
H  I  B  I  G  Z  B  E  J  Q  T  M
O  P  A  N  C  A  K  E  S  D  I  O
C  E  N  H  A  R  R  Y  X  N  V  N
F  A  N  G  S  S  S  M  U  E  X  S
L  P  I  Z  E  E  U  O  C  I  F  T
R  B  E  R  Y  H  L  P  S  R  G  E
D  E  T  E  C  T  I  V  E  F  C  R
K  D  W  D  H  S  T  N  Z  R  E  K
C  J  P  A  I  N  T  W  G  T  N  U
A  I  V  T  Y  E  L  L  O  W  E  L
L  O  R  A  N  G  E  N  N  A  T  E
B  Y  K  O  W  A  D  P  L  A  I  N
```

Name _____

Investigate My Secret Friend

Complete the paragraph that tells about a friend of yours. Then write the words in the Word List.

My friend's name is _____
(first name)

_____. He/She has
(last name)

_____ hair and
(color)

_____ eyes. _____
(color)   (friend's first name)

has _____ brother(s) and
(a number word)

_____ sister(s). He/She likes to eat
(a number word)

_____. _____ is
(favorite food)   (color)

his/her favorite color. My friend likes to _____.
(something he/she likes to do)

I know you will like _____
(friend's first name)

_____ too.
(last name)

Word List

_____   _____   _____

_____   _____   _____

_____   _____   _____

_____   _____   _____

Name _____

Investigate My Secret Friend *(cont.)*

Create your own secret friend word search puzzle. Write nine words on the lines below. Place the letters of each word that you used in your Word List in the empty spaces below. They may go up, down, across, or diagonally. Fill in the empty spaces with other letters. Exchange your puzzle with someone else. Solve each other's puzzles.

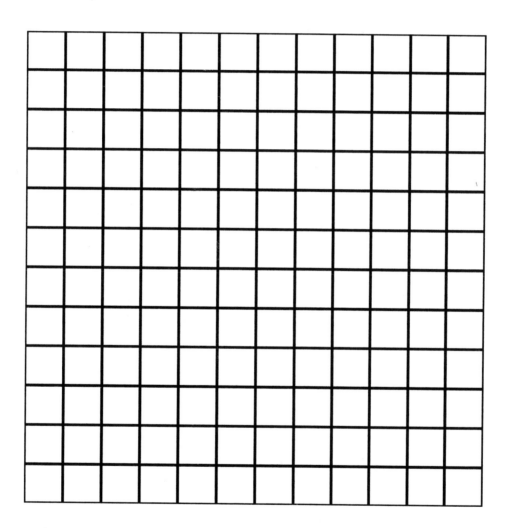

Word List

_____ _____ _____

_____ _____ _____

_____ _____ _____

Name _____

Read and Retell

Directions: Read another *Nate the Great* book and retell the story, using this activity sheet.

Title _____

Setting _____

Characters _____

_____

What mystery did Nate have to solve? _____

_____

_____

What clues helped Nate solve the case? _____

_____

_____

What part did you like the best? Why? _____

_____

_____

Draw a picture of your favorite part on the back of this paper.

Detective's Name_____

Classroom Investigation

Directions: One of the most important parts of being a good detective is asking questions. Ask your classmates the following questions. Find at least one classmate to answer "yes" to each question. When a classmate answers "yes" to a question, write his or her name on the line next to the question. When you have a name next to each question, you have completed the investigation!

1. Do you like pancakes? _____

2. Do you have a dog? _____

3. Is yellow your favorite color? _____

4. Do you write notes to your mother? _____

5. Do you have a black cat? _____

6. Would you help a good friend?_____

7. Do you eat breakfast? _____

8. Do you have a little brother?_____

9. Do you like to paint pictures? _____

10. Have you read other *Nate the Great* books? _____

    Now think of another question that you could have asked, and write here.

    _____

    _____

    _____

Name _____

Pancakes Come in Many Sizes

Directions: Measure the diameters of these pancakes in centimeters and inches. Write the diameters below each pancake. Then number them, in the centers, from the largest to the smallest, with 1 being the largest and 6 being the smallest.

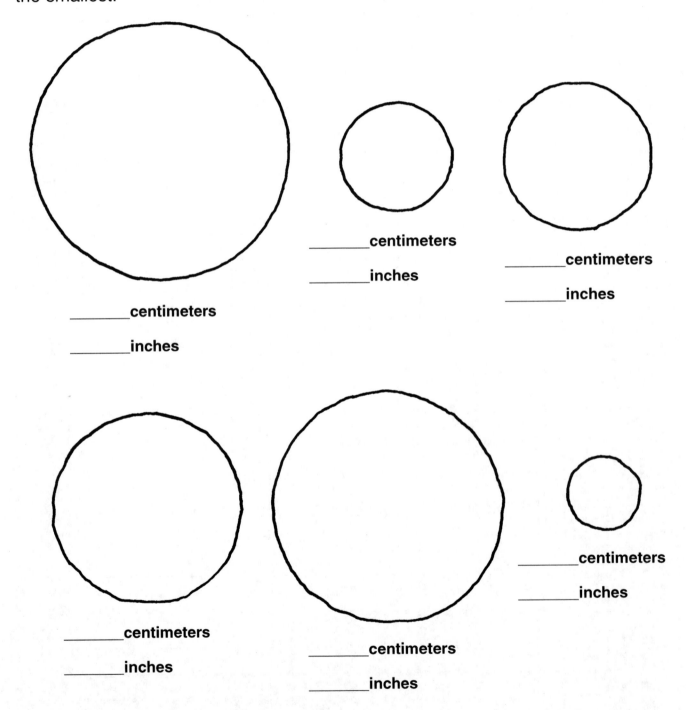

_____centimeters

_____inches

_____centimeters

_____inches

_____centimeters

_____inches

_____centimeters

_____inches

_____centimeters

_____inches

_____centimeters

_____inches

Name _____

Our Pet Pictograph

Directions: Altogether, Annie and Rosamond have five pets: a dog and four cats. How many pets do we have in our class? Complete the pictograph to represent the pets belonging to people in this classroom. Write the kind of pet on the line, and then draw one picture for each pet counted. Here are some example pictures.

dog   cat   hamster

bird   fish   lizard

Pet	How many?

Name _____

Pet Pictograph Problems

Directions: Use your completed pictograph to solve these problems. Write the answers on the lines below the problems.

There are _____ dogs and _____ birds. How many more are there of one animal than the other?

_____

There are _____ cats and _____ hamsters in the pictograph. How many are there in all?

_____

There are _____ birds, _____ cats, and _____ dogs. How many are there in all?

There are _____ fish and _____ lizards. How many more are there of one pet than the other?

_____

_____

Name _____

Piano Problems

In the first *Nate the Great* book we are introduced to Rosamond. In other *Nate the Great* books we learn that Rosamond likes to teach piano. Pretend that you are a piano teacher. Between 3:00 P.M. and 4:00 P.M. you have to give six individual piano lessons to Annie, Pip, Claude, Esmeralda, Rosamond, and Nate. How long will each lesson last? What time will each lesson begin and end? Show the starting time for each lesson on the clock and write the student's name under the clock. The first lesson will start at 3:00.

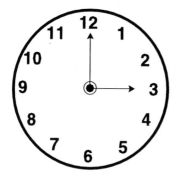

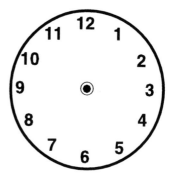

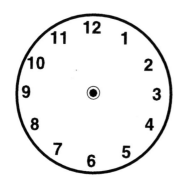

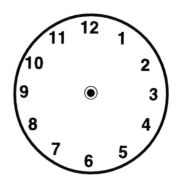

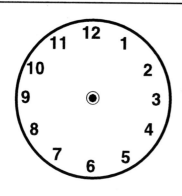

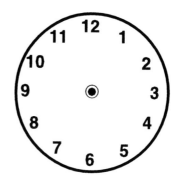

Be a Nate Songwriter

Directions: Use the example below to write a song about *Nate the Great* to the tune "Frère Jacques" or "Are You Sleeping?" Think of a simple problem to solve and its solution. Then use your ideas to write your own song.

Problem

Nate the Great,
Nate the Great,
Please help me.
Please help me.
I have lost my baseball cap.
I have lost my baseball cap.
Come right away!
Come right away!

Solution

I am Nate,
I am Nate,
And I'm great!
And I'm great!
The cap is in your book bag.
The cap is in your book bag.
The case is solved!
The case is solved!

Problem

Solution

Fascinating Fingerprints

A fingerprint is a mark made on a surface by a fingertip. It has wavy lines which are from the tiny ridges on the skin of a finger. You leave behind a small trace of who you are when you touch something. This trace is called a latent (hidden) print, and it contains dirt, oil, and perspiration. Fingerprints are visible when they are developed. No two people have the same fingerprints, and your fingerprints never change naturally. Fingerprints are sometimes used to identify people.

The three basic patterns of fingerprints are the *arch*, *loop*, and *whorl*. About 65% of the population have loops, 30% have whorls, and 5% have arches.

Arch	Loop	Whorl

An arch has lines that begin on one side, rise in the middle, come down, and leave on the other side.	A loop has lines that begin on one side, rise in the middle, make a sharp curve, and leave on the same side.	A whorl has many circles that do not leave any side of the fingerprint.

What Are Your Fingerprint Patterns?

Materials:

- scrap paper
- pencil
- clear tape
- magnifying glass
- copies of Fingerprint Fun! (pages 30 and 31)

Procedure:

1. Using a pencil, scribble a big, dark spot on a sheet of scrap paper.
2. Rub your finger back and forth across the black spot.
3. Put a piece of clear tape over the blackened part of your finger.
4. Lift off the tape. Place it on the activity sheet in the circle above the corresponding finger of the correct hand.
5. Repeat steps 1–4 for each finger.
6. Use a magnifying glass to study the different patterns.

Name _____

Fingerprint Fun!

Right Hand

Name _____

Fingerprint Fun! (cont.)

Left Hand

Experimenting with Color

Teacher Information Guide

These experiments may be done by the teacher as demonstrations or by groups of students. The students may complete the "Science Fun with Nate the Great!" form on page 33 as each step is completed.

Experiment One

Question: *How can celery change color?* Ask the students to write their reactions to this question.

Materials: three celery stalks with tops; three plastic cups or glasses; scissors; red, blue, and yellow food coloring; water; three spoons

Experiment: Fill each cup about one-third full with water. Number the cups 1 through 3. Place 14 drops of food coloring in each of the cups as follows: red in cup #1; blue in cup #2; yellow in cup #3. Stir each of the three cups. Snip off the ends of the celery stalks. Place one stalk in each cup of colored water. Observe the changes for two days.

Results: The celery tops should change color, and the stalks should be streaked with color.

Conclusions: Water rises from a plant's roots, through its stalk, and then to its leaves.

(**Note:** Three white carnations may also be used for this experiment.)

Experiment Two

Question: *What happens when you mix primary colors?* Ask the students to write their reactions to this question.

Materials: six clear plastic cups; water; spoons; red, yellow, and blue food coloring

Experiment: Fill each cup halfway with water. Number the cups 1 through 6. Place 6 drops of food coloring in each of the first 3 cups as follows: red in cup #1; blue in cup #2; yellow in cup #3. Stir each of the three cups. Then, pour some yellow water (cup #3) and 2 spoonfuls of red water (cup #1) into cup #4. Pour some red water (cup # 1) and two spoonfuls of blue water (cup #2) into cup #5. Pour some yellow water (cup #3) and two spoonfuls of blue water (cup #2) into cup #6.

Results: The water in the fourth cup will be orange. The water in the fifth cup will be purple. The water in the sixth cup will be green.

Conclusions: The secondary colors, orange, purple, and green, are each made from mixing two primary colors.

Name _____

Science Fun with Nate the Great!

Question _____

I think_____

_____

_____

Materials I used_____

_____

_____

What I did _____

_____

_____

What I saw (what happened) _____

_____

_____

_____

What I learned _____

_____

_____

_____

Pancakes Around the World

Pancakes are consumed worldwide. They are versatile and enjoyed as a basic food by many different groups of people. A basic batter recipe usually contains flour, eggs, baking powder, melted shortening, and milk or water. They can be served flat, folded, rolled and filled, or topped with meat, cheese, seafood, fruit, vegetables, jam, syrup, sweets, or anything savory. Many cultures have adjusted the basic recipe to satisfy their unique taste buds.

Discover the varieties of pancakes enjoyed by people throughout the world. Below are their names and countries of origin. They are listed in flat, rolled, and folded categories, but some may be served in more than one manner (for example, a tortilla may be served flat, rolled, or folded).

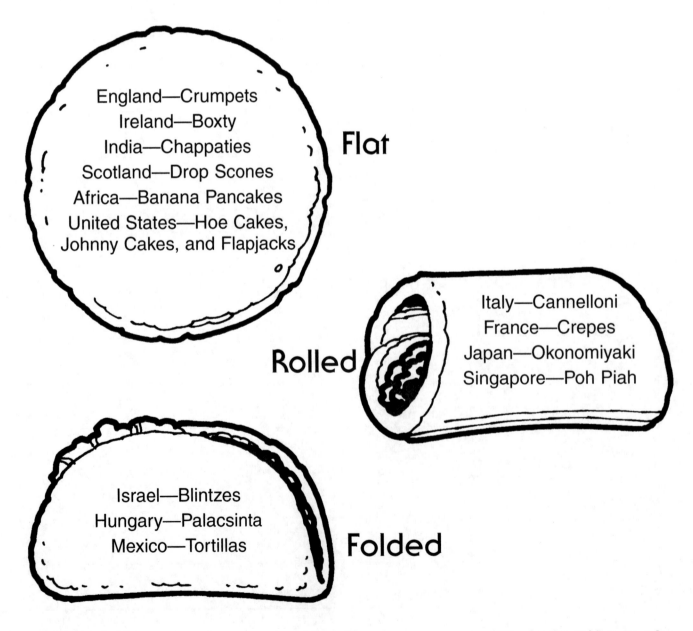

Flat

England—Crumpets
Ireland—Boxty
India—Chappaties
Scotland—Drop Scones
Africa—Banana Pancakes
United States—Hoe Cakes,
Johnny Cakes, and Flapjacks

Rolled

Italy—Cannelloni
France—Crepes
Japan—Okonomiyaki
Singapore—Poh Piah

Folded

Israel—Blintzes
Hungary—Palacsinta
Mexico—Tortillas

Pancakes Around the World— Reference Guide

——— Flat Pancakes ———

Banana Pancakes—*Africa:* A thick pancake, it is made from mealie (corn flour) and bananas.

Boxty—*Ireland:* A potato pancake, it is made from grated new potatoes and flour.

Chappaties—*India:* A thin pancake, it is used as a food and as an eating utensil to scoop up food to your mouth.

Crumpets—*England:* A light, round pancake, it is served with tea.

Drop Scones—*Scotland:* A small pancake made from oats, it is baked in an oven or cooked on a grill, and cut into fourths.

Flapjacks—*United States:* "Jack" was an old term for a half-cup liquid measure. A flapjack was a half-cup of stewed fruit inside of a pancake. Later, the fruit was left out, and flapjack became another name for pancake.

Hoe Cakes or Johnny Cakes—*United States:* In the 1800s they were called journey cakes, because they were a basic food of the settlers moving west. They were cooked on a greased, flat hoe blade over an open fire. This is why they are called hoe cakes.

——— Rolled and Filled Pancakes ———

Cannelloni—*Italy:* Squares of dough are spread with chopped chicken, meat, cheese, or a vegetable mixture and then rolled, covered with a sauce, and baked.

Crepes—*France:* A thin, rolled pancake, it is filled with fruit, seafood, or meat.

Okonomiyaki—*Japan:* A rolled pancake, it is filled with shrimp, bean sprouts, or other vegetables.

Poh Piah—*Singapore:* A rolled pancake, it is made with rice flour and water and then filled with oriental mixtures.

——— Folded and Filled Pancakes ———

Blintzes—*Israel:* A Jewish pancake, it is usually filled with cheese, lox, onions, or sweets. The four corners of the pancake are folded toward the center before cooking.

Palacsinta—*Hungary:* A dessert pancake, it is filled with fruit or sweets before folding.

Tortillas—*Mexico:* A thin pancake, it is made of mashed corn or corn flour. They are filled with a variety of ingredients which may include meat, beans, rice, and/or vegetables.

Detective's Name _____

The Case of the Popular Pancake

You are on a case to find a popular pancake somewhere in the world. You may investigate one from "Pancakes Around the World" or one of your own choosing. As you set out to solve your case, answer the questions below. When you are finished, share your case with a friend.

1. What is the pancake's name? _____

2. How is it prepared? _____

_____

_____

3. In what country is it eaten? _____

4. Is it eaten for breakfast, lunch, and/or dinner? _____

5. Why do people enjoy it? _____

_____

6. What did you learn about this country? Include important facts about the country. (If you need more writing space, use the back of this paper.)

_____

_____

_____

If possible, have someone at home help you prepare this pancake.

Name _____

A Color Wheel Pancake

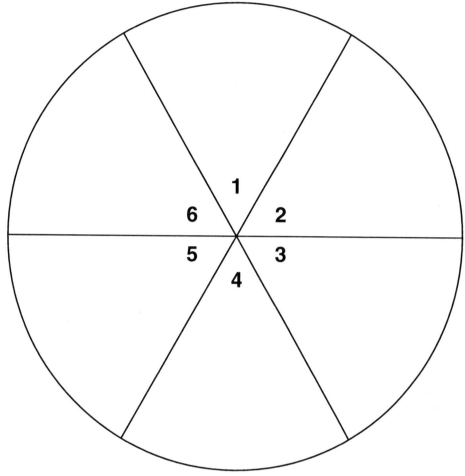

- Primary colors are colors from which other colors are made. Color sections 1, 3, and 5 of the pancake with the primary colors as directed.

    Section 1—yellow   Section 3—red   Section 5—blue

- Secondary colors are colors that are mixed from two primary colors. Color sections 2, 4, and 6 of the pancake with the secondary colors as directed.

    Section 2—orange   Section 4—purple   Section 6—green

- Complete the following color equations.

    _____+_____ = orange

    _____+_____ = purple

    _____+_____ = green

- On the other side of this paper, draw, color, and label things that are primary and secondary colors.

Name _____

Nate Needs Some New Clothes!

Directions: Nate always wears the same clothes when he is out on a case. Create a new outfit for him, using different colors and designs. Label any interesting features or details of his new outfit.

When you are finished with Nate's new clothes, draw Sludge, his dog (introduced in later books in the *Nate the Great* series), and give him a new dog collar.

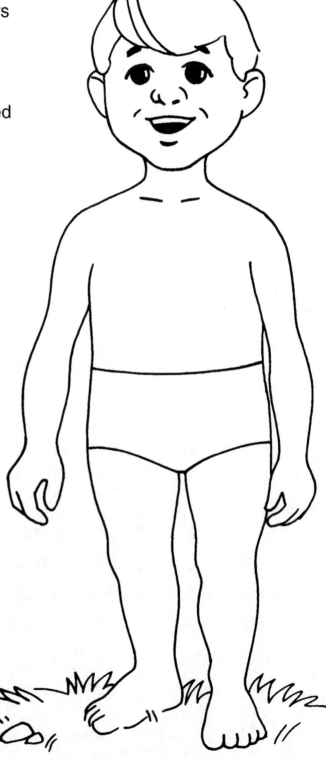

Name _____

Super, Big, Little, and Plain

Directions: Rosamond's cats are named Super Hex, Big Hex, Little Hex, and Plain Hex. In the circles below, draw or list things that are super, big, or little in size, and also things that are plain in appearance.

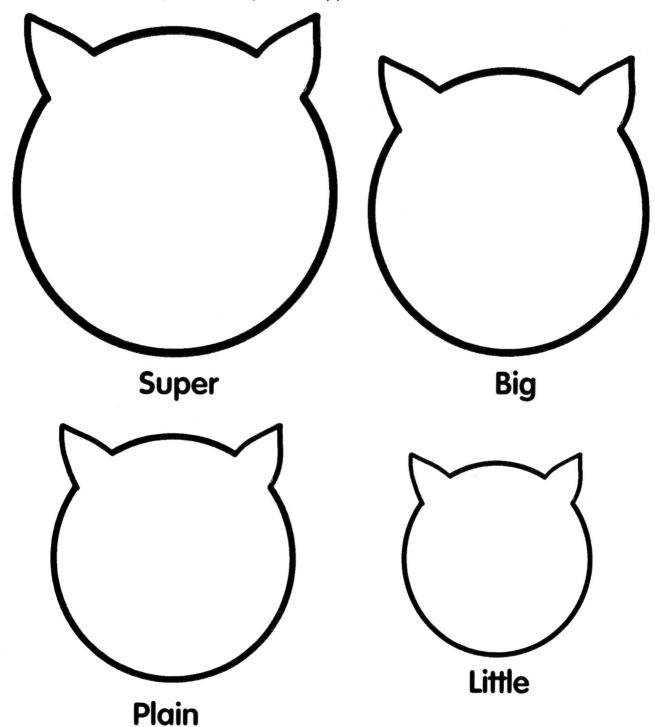

Super

Big

Plain

Little

Name _____

New Character Clues

Directions: Every time you are introduced to a new character in your reading, fill out a copy of this page.

_____is a new character in this book. This is what
    (name)
I learned about _____. _____
                        (her/him)

_____

_____

_____

_____

I _____ like _____ as
        (would/would not)   *(character's name)*
a friend, because_____.

A Picture ID of_____
                              (name)

Draw a picture of this character for identification.

Readers' Theater Script

Characters

Narrator 1	Rosamond	Annie
Narrator 2	Nate	Harry
Narrator 3		

Narrator 1: Nate the Great had just finished his favorite breakfast of juice, milk, and a stack of pancakes, when the telephone rang. It was his friend, Annie.

Annie: Oh Nate, please help me! My favorite picture is missing, and I can't find it! It is urgent! I need your help right away!

Nate: I will be there as soon as I put on my detective uniform and write a note to my mother so that she knows I'm on a case.

Narrator 2: Nate really liked his friend Annie, so he hurried to her house. When he arrived, Annie was eating pancakes too!

Annie: Oh, I'm glad you're here! Yesterday I painted a great portrait of Fang, my dog. I left it on the desk in my room to dry. Today it is gone!

Nate: Hmmm. This sounds very interesting. Let's go to your room.

Narrator 3: When they got to Annie's room, everything was yellow . . . the walls, the bed, the chair, and the desk.

Narrator 1: Nate looked everywhere in the room, and all he found was a picture of a red dog in the wastebasket. Annie's painting was yellow.

Nate: Annie, did you show your picture to anyone?

Annie: Yes. I showed it to Rosamond, my friend; Harry, my brother; and Fang, my dog.

Nate: Hmmm, tell me about Fang.

Annie: Well, he is very big, and he has very big teeth . . . but he doesn't bite. Do you want to see him?

Nate: Yes, let's go out to the yard.

Narrator 2: They went to the yard and visited Fang, who was busy burying a bone. Nate got the idea that Fang may have buried the picture.

Narrator 3: Annie and Nate dug for two hours, but only found worms, ants, bones, and rocks. So they decided to go back to Annie's house, eat pancakes, and discuss the case.

Nate: These pancakes have given me an idea. Let's go to Rosamond's house and talk to her.

Narrator 1: Rosamond loved cats and had four black cats with green eyes: Super Hex, Big Hex, Little Hex, and Plain Hex. She was happy to see Nate and Annie.

Readers' Theater Script *(cont.)*

Rosamond: Oh! I am so glad that you came over! I need a detective to find Super Hex! He is lost!

Narrator 2: They went into Rosamond's house and looked around. Then they sat down and Big Hex jumped on Nate's lap. Immediately, Nate and Big Hex did not like each other.

Nate: Annie, we have got to leave now.

Narrator 3: As Nate stood up, he tripped over Super Hex's big, long tail! He had been hiding under Nate's chair.

Rosamond: Oh Nate, you are such a great detective! Thank you for finding Super Hex!

Narrator 1: As they left, Nate was convinced that Rosamond did not take Fang's picture. She only liked cats. The next suspect would be Annie's little brother, Harry.

Narrator 2: When they saw Harry, he was covered with red paint. He liked to paint.

Harry: Look! Me paint a monster with three heads, a house, a tree, and a clown!

Narrator 3: Harry had also painted the doorknob, a slipper, and part of the wall. All of a sudden, Nate had solved the problem.

Nate: I have found Fang's picture right here on the wall.

Annie: I don't see it.

Nate: Well, there are three pictures that are red, but the monster with three heads is orange. The yellow paint on your dog's picture was not dry when Harry painted the red monster over it. Red and yellow make orange, and that is why the monster is orange.

Annie: Wow! I do see that two of the heads were Fang's ears, and the other head was his tail. Harry, I am angry with you for ruining my picture! Nate, how can I thank you for solving the case?

Nate: Let's all have some pancakes.

Annie: Nate, guess what. Tomorrow I am going to paint a new picture! Please come back and see it.

Nate: You'd better be sure that Harry doesn't see it first.

Harry: You can say that again!

Everyone: They all smiled at each other. After the pancakes were gone, Nate said good-bye and walked home in the rain feeling happy.

Bibliography

Other *Nate the Great* Books

Author: Marjorie Weinman Sharmat

Nate the Great and the Lost List. Bantam Doubleday Dell Books for Young Readers, 1981.

Nate the Great and the Phony Clue. Bantam Doubleday Dell Books for Young Readers, 1981.

Nate the Great and the Sticky Case. Dell Publishing Co., Inc., 1981.

Nate the Great and the Missing Key. Bantam Doubleday Dell Books for Young Readers, 1982.

Nate the Great and the Snowy Trail. Bantam Doubleday Dell Books for Young Readers, 1984.

Nate the Great and the Fishy Prize. Bantam Doubleday Dell Books for Young Readers, 1988.

Nate the Great Goes Undercover. The Putnam Publishing Group, 1989.

Nate the Great and the Stupidweed. Bantam Doubleday Dell Books for Young Readers, 1989.

Nate the Great and the Boring Beach Bag. Bantam Doubleday Dell Books for Young Readers, 1989.

Nate the Great and the Halloween Hunt. Bantam Doubleday Dell Books for Young Readers, 1990.

Nate the Great Goes Down in the Dumps. Dell Publishing Co., Inc., 1991.

Nate the Great and the Stolen Base. Dell Publishing Co., Inc., 1994.

Nate the Great and the Mushy Valentine. Dell Publishing Co., Inc., 1995.

Nate the Great Saves the King of Sweden. Bantam Doubleday Dell Books, 1997

Authors: Marjorie Weinman Sharmat and Rosalind Weinman

Nate the Great and the Pillowcase. Bantam Doubleday Dell Books for Young Readers, 1995.

Authors: Marjorie Weinman Sharmat and Craig Sharmat

Nate the Great and the Musical Note. Dell Publishing Co., Inc., 1991.

Nate the Great and the Crunchy Christmas. Delacorte Press Books, 1996.

Nate the Great and the Tardy Tortoise. Dell Publishing Co., Inc., 1997.

Foreign Distributors

For Bantam Doubleday Dell Books for Young Readers, Dell Publishing Co., Inc., or Delecorte Press Books:

   Canada—Doubleday Dell Seal
   UK—Bantam Doubleday Dell
   AUS—Transworld Publishers

For The Putnam Publishing Group:

   Canada—BeJo Sales
   UK and AUS—Warner International

Bibliography *(cont.)*

Related Books About Color

Ehlert, Lois. *Color Zoo.* J.B. Lippincott, 1989.

Heller, Ruth. *Color.* Putnam and Grosset, 1995.

Jonas, Ann. *Color Dance.* Greenwillow Books, 1989.

Kaler, Rebecca. *Blueberry Bear.* Inquiring Voices Press, 1993.

Walsh, Ellen. *Mouse Paint.* Harcourt Brace Jovanovich, 1989.

Related Pancake Books (Books with Pancake Recipes)

Alston, Elizabeth. *Pancakes and Waffles.* HarperCollins, 1993.

Brown, Karen. *Kids are Cookin'.* Meadowbrook Press, New York, 1997.

Cunningham, Marion. *Cooking with Children.* Alfred A. Knopf, 1995.

Miller, Justin. *Cooking with Justin.* Andrews and McMeel, Kansas City, 1997.

Zabriskie, George and Sherry LaFollette. *The Great Pancake Cookbook.* Contemporary Books, 1985.

Audio-Visual Materials

Listening Library Inc.
One Park Avenue
Old Greenwich, CT 06870-1727
1-800-243-4504
FAX 1-800-454-0606

Books with Cassettes
Nate the Great (18 minutes) WFTR 93 SP

Nate the Great Goes Undercover (19 minutes) WFTR 172 SP

Nate the Great and the Halloween Hunt (21 minutes) WFTR 170 SP

Nate the Great and the Missing Key (19 minutes) WFTR 75 SP

Appendix

Here are some activity ideas for your students for other *Nate the Great* titles.

Nate the Great Goes Undercover

1. Discuss and write clues about the three new characters in this book, Esmeralda, Oliver, and Sludge. Use the activity "New Character Clues" on page 40.
2. Research animals that go out at night (cats, rats, bats, mice, shrews, skunks, raccoons, moles, opossums, etc.).
3. Copy one of Nate's notes in your neatest handwriting.
4. Inquire and study about the disposal and recycling of garbage and refuse in your community.

Nate the Great and the Lost List

1. Discuss and write clues about the new character, Claude, who appears in this book. Use the activity "New Character Clues" on page 40.
2. Pretend you are shopping at the supermarket. Create a grocery list.
3. Draw a map of the street on which your home or school is located.
4. Experiment to find out which way the wind is blowing on a windy day. Drop a piece of paper and watch which direction it moves.
5. Pretend you are planning a cat party. Discuss what food, games, prizes, and other activities will be included.

Nate the Great and the Phony Clue

1. Discuss and write clues about the new characters, Finley and Pip, who appear in this book. Use the activity "New Character Clues" on page 40.
2. Brainstorm a list of words that have "vita" at the beginning, middle, or end.
3. Write a note to a friend. Tear it into six pieces. Exchange it with the friend to put back together again and then read.
4. Try this science experiment. On a piece of paper, write "Phony Clue" with permanent markers. Wet the paper, turn it over, and observe the two words written backwards. Is this really a phony clue? Refer to the activity "Science Fun with Nate the Great!" on page 33.
5. Write an invitation to a friend.

Nate the Great and the Sticky Case

1. Research the stegosaurus and other dinosaurs. Share the information that you learn.
2. Design a dinosaur stamp.
3. Press the dry sole of a shoe onto the sticky side of a self-adhesive stamp or sticker. Observe what happens. Then, wet the sole of another shoe and press it onto the sticky side of a regular stamp or sticker. Observe what happens. Refer to the activity "Science Fun with Nate the Great!" on page 33.

Appendix *(cont.)*

Nate the Great and the Missing Key

1. In your community, inquire about how to get a dog license.
2. Design different keys.
3. List and discuss the many uses for keys.
4. Play "Hide the Key." Hide a key in the room. Then write a poem which gives clues about where it is.
5. Brainstorm a list of items that are shiny and silvery.

Nate the Great and the Snowy Trail

1. If you live in a place with a snowy climate, play a modern version of "Fox and Geese." Follow a footprint trail made by your friends.
2. Observe and discuss how mathematical terms are included in this story. (1 hour, old, July 12, light, heavy, big, small, medium, square, pointy, flat, four, wide circle, high, six, two, etc.)
3. Write a story about the most beautiful birthday gift that you have ever received.
4. Use the stick puppets on pages 16 and 17 to act out this story.
5. Write what you think happened to Super Duper Hex at the end of the story, and continue the cat's experiences.

Nate the Great and the Fishy Prize

1. Discuss Nate's ingredients for pancakes—flour, eggs, butter, milk, salt, sugar, and baking powder—and their purposes as he completes his supermarket purchases.
2. Pancakes come in different sizes. Complete the activity "Pancakes Come in Many Sizes" on page 24.
3. Create a chart displaying the pets signed up for the contest.
4. Recycle and decorate a can.
5. Have a class Pet Fair.

Nate the Great Stalks Stupidweed

1. Find something for the class to adopt for the school year, such as a tree, a school sign, a flower garden, playground equipment, etc.
2. Research different kinds of weeds.
3. Compare and contrast weeds with useful plants, such as flowers, vegetables, grass, herbs, etc.
4. Brainstorm a list of ways to either safely eliminate or find effective uses for weeds.
5. At the end of this book, Nate visited the library and took out a book called *The Weed Killer*. Create a story about a "weed killer."

Nate the Great and the Boring Beach Bag

1. Pretend you are going to the beach for the day. Write about or draw pictures of what you would take with you.
2. Design a beach bag, a beach ball, a beach towel, or a bathing suit.
3. Create a menu for a beachside food stand.
4. Brainstorm ideas about what you can make or do with sand.

Appendix *(cont.)*

Nate the Great Goes Down in the Dumps

1. Write a story about what you think will happen in the future.
2. Have a Box Fair. Everyone brings a box. Each box has a label on it that tells what it contains. Share and discuss the boxes, their contents, and labels.
3. Recycle a throw-away box, and turn it into something useful. Display your creation at a Box Exhibit.
4. Design and create some new clothes for Nate. Complete the activity "Nate Needs Some New Clothes!" on page 38.
5. Visit a recycling center or have an employee from the center talk to the class.

Nate the Great and the Halloween Hunt

1. Copy Nate's note to his mother in your neatest handwriting.
2. Write a story or a poem about "The Haunted House."
3. Share a time when you were scared.
4. Write and share new trick-or-treat rhymes. Then decorate trick-or-treat bags.
5. Brainstorm a list of ideas that might help Nate solve the unsolved mystery at the end.

Nate the Great and the Musical Note

1. Write a riddle about some aspect of music, and share it with a friend.
2. Draw a picture of the piano keys that Rosamond used when she played the scale in this order, C, D, E, F, G, A, and B. Refer to Nate's drawing in the book.
3. Rosamond needs an appointment book to schedule her lessons. Help her by completing the activity "Piano Problems" on page 27.

Nate the Great and the Stolen Base

1. Research more information about Babe Ruth or other famous baseball players.
2. Read and share baseball trading cards.
3. Use a 3" x 5" (7.62 x 12.7 cm) index card to create a trading card that has your picture and tells about you.
4. Investigate the characteristics of an octopus.

Nate the Great and the Pillowcase

1. Design some new clothes for Fang.
2. Brainstorm and discuss the different kinds of pillows and their uses.
3. Write a story about your favorite pillow.
4. Use the puppets on pages 16 and 17 to act out this story.
5. Rosamond has four cats with the last name Hex. Complete the activity about Rosamond's cats. (page 39)

Appendix *(cont.)*

Nate the Great and the Mushy Valentine

1. Design your own valentine.
2. Brainstorm a list of rhyming words. Write valentine verses.
3. Use letter stencils to write a note to your friend.
4. Make a list of the initials of everyone in the class. Then, randomly reread them and guess to whom they belong.

Nate the Great and the Tardy Tortoise

1. Research and learn more about tortoises and other reptiles.
2. Write math story problems about Speedy, the hungry tortoise and Nate's disappearing garden flowers.
3. Brainstorm a list of unique pets that some people own.
4. Invite a veterinarian to speak to the class about his or her career.
5. Use the puppets on pages 16 and 17 to act out this story.

Nate the Great and the Crunchy Christmas

1. Create a Christmas card to send to Fang.
2. Invite a postal carrier to visit your class and discuss his or her career.
3. Collect different kinds of catalogs. Read and discuss their similarities and differences.
4. Discuss and write rebus sentences or words.
5. Learn more about the Jewish holiday Chanukah or Hanukkah.

Nate the Great Saves the King of Sweden

1. Locate Scandinavia and learn more about its countries: Sweden, Norway, Denmark, Finland, and sometimes Iceland.
2. Create a picture postcard of your favorite place.
3. Collect foreign stamps and compare them to stamps from the United States.
4. Pretend that you are going to Sweden for one week. Plan what you would take in one suitcase. On a piece of paper, draw the items you would take.
5. Learn more about trolls and their lifestyles and habits.
6. Design a bookmark with one or more trolls on it.